Bible Reader's Series

A Study of Jeremiah

LOOKING FOR A NEW DAY

J. Ellsworth Kalas

Abingdon Press / Nashville

LOOKING FOR A NEW DAY
A STUDY OF JEREMIAH

Lessons are based on the International Sunday School Lessons for Christian Teaching, copyright © 1984, by the Committee on the Uniform
Series. Text excerpted from *Adult Bible Studies*, Fall 1988.

This book is printed on acid-free, elemental chlorine-free paper.

ISBN 0-687-07458-4
ISBN 978-0-687-07458-7

07 08 09 10 11 12—10 9 8 7 6 5 4 3 2
Manufactured in the United States of America.

CONTENTS

Chapter One

RESPONDING TO GOD'S CALL

PURPOSE

To recognize that just as Jeremiah was called in his time to declare a new day, we are called to bring God's hope to our time

BIBLE PASSAGE

Jeremiah 1:4-10, 17-19

4 Now the word of the LORD came to me saying,

5 "Before I formed you in the womb
>   I knew you,
> and before you were born
>   I consecrated you;
> I appointed you a prophet to the nations."

6 Then I said, "Ah, Lord GOD! Truly I do not know how to speak, for I am only a boy."   7 But the LORD said to me,

> "Do not say, 'I am only a boy';
> for you shall go to all to whom
>   I send you,
> and you shall speak whatever
>   I command you,

8 Do not be afraid of them,
> for I am with you to deliver you,
>   says the LORD."

9 Then the LORD put out his hand and touched my mouth; and the LORD said to me,
"Now I have put my words in
        your mouth.
10 See, today I appoint you over
            nations and over kingdoms,
    to pluck up and to pull down,
    to destroy and to overthrow,
    to build and to plant.". . .
17 But you, gird up your loins; stand up and tell them everything that I command you. Do not break down before them, or I will break you before them.   18 And I for my part have made you today a fortified city, an iron pillar, and a bronze wall, against the whole land—against the kings of Judah, its princes, its priests, and the people of the land. 19 They will fight against you; but they shall not prevail against you, for I am with you, says the LORD, to deliver you.

CORE VERSES

The word of the LORD came to me, saying,
"Before I formed you in the womb
    I knew you,
and before you were born
    I consecrated you;
I appointed you a prophet to the nations."
                                    (Jeremiah 1:4-5)

OUR NEED

God always has called us to service, throughout the Old Testament and the New, and even today. The God we serve has pursued the human race since we began our wanderings. To follow such a God surely must mean that we, too, will feel called to serve the human race God loves so clearly.

God's call always is a solicitation, not a demand. The call may be so convincing that it is hard to resist and so insistent that we wonder if we can escape it. Nevertheless, it is ours to accept or to reject.

In practice, however, we probably accept only a measure of our calling. I doubt that we ever comprehend its full potential. Dwight L. Moody, a nineteenth-century evangelist, said that the world had yet to see what God could do with people who would give themselves fully to God's will and that he intended to be one of those persons. No doubt he came closer to that goal than most of us do, but I suspect that no human being ever fully fulfills that goal. Yet the call is present, and it is our choice whether to respond.

Jeremiah had his opportunity to respond to God's call more than twenty-five centuries ago. The same opportunity comes in our day.

FAITHFUL LIVING

Someone has called Jeremiah "the supreme saint of the Old Testament." Certainly few people, if any, ministered in more difficult times or were entrusted with a more unpleasant assignment. At times, Jeremiah lost heart. He felt in some dark hours that God had betrayed or forsaken him. Yet, in the end, Jeremiah's faith carried him to victory.

When we go through life's darkest passages, we need some sure point of reference. We would prefer that we had a light to show us the way into the future. Since we do not have such a light, it is reassuring if we can recall some experience in the past that will remind us of God's strength and mercy. A friend once told me of the fear he felt as a boy when he had to make a nighttime run from the farmhouse to the barn. The dark barn held no promise, so he would turn around at intervals to see the lights in the kitchen window. He could not see what was ahead, but he could look back to the light. Jeremiah's call must have served that purpose in his life often.

The call had come on a bright, promising day. Jeremiah grew up in the priestly city of Anathoth, the son of a priest with the same prospect for his life. Though the nation had endured a long period of religious denial under King Manasseh, King Josiah brought a happy change. "While he was still a boy, [Josiah] began to seek the God of his ancestor David" (2 Chronicles 34:3). Josiah soon began a vigorous reform, tearing down pagan altars and dramatically demonstrating to the people that he wanted the nation to return to God.

Then Josiah commanded some of the priests to begin repairing the Temple; for during the years when the nation had flirted with pagan gods, they had neglected the Temple. Now came the most significant event of all. During this major housecleaning, workers found a lost copy of the law, probably the Book of Deuteronomy. When Shaphan read the law to Josiah, he called the entire nation to repentance.

What events of the past remind you to stay on the right track?

Superficial Change

Jeremiah was a young man during this period of remarkable religious stirring. As he watched the older priests implement reform, he rejoiced in what was happening. Perhaps he envied them their opportunity to lead the nation back to God.

Yet as time went by, Jeremiah must have perceived that all was not well. As we shall learn in more detail in a later chapter, the spiritual awakening apparently did not spread widely through the nation, nor did it reach a level of transforming depth. A movement that should have revolutionized a generation for God became instead a deep stirring for a few and a superficial, fleeting excitement for the larger populace.

You and I can read this story with special empathy. Today many people feel that we are living in a time of religious awakening. Yet with all the prominence the electronic media and well-known personalities from politics, sports, and entertainment give to the gospel, it seems to have had little impact on the lifestyle of the general public.

What similarities do you see between the revival in Josiah's time and the religious renewal in our day?

The Setting for a Call

God's work in our personal life always comes within some general context. Spiritual experience does not occur in a vacuum. For Jeremiah, the call came in the setting of Josiah's reform, the discovery of the book of the law, and the incomplete renewal that followed.

Jeremiah lived in a time of great promise but also of a growing fear of disappointment. On the one hand, he probably felt inferior to his elders, people who had counseled with the king and who had proved their integrity during the years of King Manasseh. On the other hand, he must have experienced increasing apprehension as he watched the spirit of renewal dissipate.

Then the word of God came to Jeremiah:

> **Before I formed you in the womb**
> **I knew you,**
> **and before you were born**
> **I consecrated you;**
> **I appointed you a prophet to the nations.**
> **(Jeremiah 1:5)**

How does one small human being respond when God says, "I've had you in my plans for a long time, since even before you were born"? From our vantage point, looking at the story from an objective distance, we might imagine the exultation Jeremiah felt at being so singularly chosen. Yet Jeremiah felt otherwise, and so would you and I if we were the person at issue.

God's Long-range Plans

When you and I are praying for God to intervene in matters that concern us, we often wonder why it takes so long. God is always at work behind the scenes, however, as he was in this instance. In some of Judah's darkest days, when many of the faithful no doubt cried, "Where are you, God?" God was preparing Jeremiah. What Jeremiah did was not only crucial to his generation in his nation's most painful time of upheaval; his message and the power of his personal witness still are with us today, more than twenty-five centuries later.

If we believe that God is all-knowing, it follows that God knows the future as well. Yet if God knows the future, is the future already settled and determined? I do not worry unduly about this issue because I have concluded that my powers of reasoning may not be adequate to comprehend all the ways of the Divine. Yet I do find a special peace in the idea that God sees farther ahead than I do. When I read of God saying to Jeremiah, "Before I formed you in the womb, I knew you," I feel wonderfully reassured. God is looking ahead. I may become bogged down with the pain and confinement of the present, but God has a longer view. Better yet, God is at work laying a foundation for the future.

What experience in your life demonstrates that God was at work prior to your need?

Jeremiah's Response

We sometimes condemn ourselves for our reluctance to respond positively to God's call. We can find consolation in so many of our spiritual predecessors in the Bible. Jeremiah was cautious, unsure, and apologetic. "I do not know how to speak, for I am only a boy," he said (Jeremiah 1:6).

On the one hand, this response was proper. After all, who is qualified to accept a divine assignment? If Jeremiah had leaped forward and announced confidently, "You have the right person!" it would have been an act of arrogance. He had an appropriate sense of the enormity of the task and of his own limitations. And yes, he was right in raising questions about his age. In most circumstances we need experience and seasoning.

On the other hand, Jeremiah's very reluctance was a kind of arrogance. Who was he, after all, to question the wisdom of God? If God thought he was able to do the job, that should have settled the matter. In other words, what we sometimes think of as humility may be only a lack of faith in the judgment of God.

You and I often are inclined to fence God in because of our unbelief or because we are conditioned by the conventions and opinions of society. I remember a woman who lived a generation ago who felt called to preach. At the time, most of the established denominations offered virtually no opportunities for women pastors; and to make matters worse, her formal education was limited. She argued with God for some time, suggesting several men and several better trained persons before she at last gave in to the call and to the wisdom of God.

God's Response to Jeremiah

God directly and sharply contradicted Jeremiah. "Do not say, 'I am only a boy' " (Jeremiah 1:7). Some of the excuses we offer God, sincere though they may be, reflect on God's judgment. God rightly might have said, "Don't you think I know how old you are? Don't you suppose I took that into consideration when I called you?"

Indeed, in some instances the factors we see as impediments may be advantages in God's sight. When Jeremiah said that he was too young, God might have answered, "You are still young enough to be daring." When someone says he or she is too old, God may reply, "You are old enough to know the pitfalls." When we say we are too tired, God may answer, "If you are tired, lean on me."

God never means to contradict us when we voice our sincere concerns. We need to hear more than, "I know better." We need some touch from heaven. God gave Jeremiah that touch.

Jeremiah had complained that he could not speak, so God touched his mouth. "Now I have put my words in your mouth" (Jeremiah 1:9). As I understand it, Jeremiah's problem was not a speech impediment; it was the feeling that he lacked the experience and maturity to merit a hearing.

God probably grants the special touch of reassurance at the times when we feel most inadequate. On the other hand, God may be as close at other times; but we are too absorbed in ourselves to hear God's voice or to feel God's touch.

In what ways have you limited God's effectiveness in your life?

The Daring Assignment

If Jeremiah could have anticipated all that was ahead of him, he might have argued with God still longer. Yet while the Bible does not describe specifically the years of rejection and persecution, the nature of Jeremiah's call hinted strongly that he was headed for no ordinary assignment. "See, today I appoint you over nations and over kingdoms," God said (Jeremiah 1:10). Jeremiah was not only to preach to them, as indicated in the initial word; his role contained a quality of dominance. By speaking the word of God, Jeremiah would be challenging and directing the nations. They would reject him at their peril, for God had authorized his declaration.

The rulers of this world march with pomp and circumstance. With so many people paying attention to their desires and with so many daily evidences of their power, they easily may forget that they are mortals who draw each breath by divine grant. The person who speaks for God, as Jeremiah did, or who lives with committed integrity, as do millions of God's humble people, possesses an inner power that any king or president might envy.

Destroy and Build

God called Jeremiah to pluck up and break down, to destroy and overthrow. If Jeremiah had been the kind of person who enjoyed pronouncing thundering judgment, God could not have used him for this task. Persons who declare judgment with relish do not speak for God, for God speaks from a broken heart.

Fortunately, Jeremiah's message was not to be judgment alone. He was privileged also "to build and to plant" (Jeremiah 1:10). Demolition should not be an end in itself but simply a clearing of rubble in order to raise a new and better structure. The tearing down of the Babylonian invasion would come in Jeremiah's time. Unfortunately, he would not see the eventual restoration.

Jeremiah's ministry was to be a difficult one, but God was going to make him "a fortified city" (Jeremiah 1:18). God assured Jeremiah that though princes, priests, and people might fight against him, they would not prevail; "for I am with you, says the LORD, to deliver you" (1:19).

What task do you feel you have to do for God at this time in history?

CLOSING PRAYER
Grant us, dear God, the grace to fulfill your purposes in our time, as Jeremiah did in his. In Jesus' name we pray. Amen.

Chapter Two

Hiding Behind Religion

PURPOSE

To learn that true worship of God must begin with repentance and a change of heart

BIBLE PASSAGE

Jeremiah 7:1-15

1 The word that came to Jeremiah from the LORD: 2 Stand in the gate of the Lord's house, and proclaim there this word, and say, Hear the word of the LORD, all you people of Judah, you that enter these gates to worship the LORD. 3 Thus says the LORD of hosts, the God of Israel: Amend your ways and your doings, and let me dwell with you in this place.   4 Do not trust in these deceptive words: "This is the temple of the LORD, the temple of the LORD, the temple of the LORD."

5 For if you truly amend your ways and your doings, if you truly act justly one with another,   6 if you do not oppress the alien, the orphan, and the widow, or shed innocent blood in this place, and if you do not go after other gods to your own hurt,   7 then I will dwell with you in this place, in the land that I gave of old to your ancestors forever and ever.

8 Here you are, trusting in deceptive words to no avail. 9 Will you steal, murder, commit adultery, swear falsely, make offerings to Baal, and go after other gods that you have not known, 10 and then come and stand before me in this house, which is called by my name, and say, "We are safe!"—only to go on doing all these abominations? 11 Has this house, which is called by my name, become a den of robbers in your sight? You know, I too am watching, says the LORD. 12 Go now to my place that was in Shiloh, where I made my name dwell at first, and see what I did to it for the wickedness of my people Israel. 13 And now, because you have done all these things, says the LORD, and when I spoke to you persistently, you did not listen, and when I called you, you did not answer, 14 therefore I will do to the house that is called by my name, in which you trust, and to the place that I gave to you and to your ancestors, just what I did to Shiloh. 15 And I will cast you out of my sight, just as I cast out all your kinsfolk, all the offspring of Ephraim.

CORE VERSE

This is the nation that did not obey the voice of the LORD their God, and did not accept discipline; truth has perished; it is cut off from their lips. (Jeremiah 7:28)

OUR NEED

The purpose of religion is to lead and to bind us to God. Unfortunately, we human beings have a peculiar ability to pervert life's purposes. We manage often to use religion to hide ourselves from God.

In a sense, that behavior is not too surprising for religion in general. After all, most primitive and pagan religions have sought either to use whatever gods the people worshiped or to protect the people from the anger of their gods. In such religions, persons gave little or no thought to moral or ethical responsibility. In truth, the aim of these religions was to hold the gods at some sort of safe distance.

The Jews in Old Testament times and we Christians are always in danger of slipping into the same patterns of thought. God seeks a people who will worship in spirit and in truth, but we tend to look for pleasing rituals through which we can avoid soul searching. God wants a people with whom he can commune; but we, at least at times, want a God who will grant us the favors we request. God hopes for a people who will minister in his name and spirit to the poor, the forsaken, and the lonely; but we look for a religion that will make us comfortable.

The words of the prophet Jeremiah may be twenty-five centuries old, but they are not out of date. If we are reasonably sensitive, they prick our conscience with the realization that we need the message as much as the people in Jeremiah's day did. False religion, or true religion misused, uses the trappings of religion to hold God at a distance. Biblical faith lays the soul bare before God so that we may find true communion.

FAITHFUL LIVING

When God called Jeremiah, he objected that he could not speak. Rather early in Jeremiah's prophetic ministry, however, God asked him to speak at a time and place that confirmed his worst fears. In that setting he justifiably could have said to God, "I told you I wasn't up to this job!"

God said, "Stand in the gate of the LORD's house" (Jeremiah 7:2). A prophet could deliver his message in no more appropriate place. The place was even more appropriate when the prophet was also a priest, as was Jeremiah.

Jeremiah's message was not the kind people expected or wanted to hear. "Do not trust," the message said, "in these deceptive words: 'This is the temple of the LORD, the temple of the LORD, the temple of the LORD!'" (7:4). At the focal point of their religious life, the prophet was to tell them, in mocking language, that they had misplaced their confidence.

Obviously God meant for the message to sting. Speaking the phrase three times was the same as chiding, "You're always saying . . ." And no doubt they were, especially since they had restored the building.

In a way, the message seems unnecessarily cruel. After all, the people had reason to feel pride in the job they had done in overcoming the neglect of past generations. As a pastor who has worked with congregations in building and remodeling programs, I know what a feeling of accomplishment a people can have in a job well done. Can we blame the people if they said, "Isn't it beautiful!" and "This is our Temple"? Why was God angry with a pride that seems so justified?

At what occasion have you found yourself indulging in similar feelings?

A Wrong Focus

Loving the Temple was not wrong. I doubt, even, that a certain quality of pride was particularly evil. Yet it was wrong for the people to think that God's house would save them. This attitude was a violation of the second commandment. That is, they had made the Temple a graven image. They had come to feel the building itself had the power to ensure the blessing of God for them.

All of us are somewhat susceptible to this temptation. At one time, I preached in a building that was awe inspiring in its French Gothic massiveness. I am sure that some of my parishioners occasionally confused the building with God. I also have known people who were attached equally to a tiny country church. They felt that if they ever left their building, they would be leaving God.

In truth, knowing where to draw the line is difficult. We ought to love our church building and to maintain it with pride. I think we are right in sensing that we approach God more easily in a church than anywhere else, precisely because it is a building that has been dedicated to God and has been immersed in hymns, prayer, and the Scripture. Yet we should not think that the building itself will save us. We dare not make it into a graven image.

How do you draw the line between loving a church building and making it an object of worship?

Deceptive Words

"Here you are, trusting in deceptive words," Jeremiah said, "to no avail" (Jeremiah 7:8). The prophet listed six of the ten commandments the people were willfully and wantonly breaking, after which they would "come and stand before me in this house, which is called by my name, and say, 'We are safe!'" (7:10).

The irony, in other words, was that they were desecrating so easily the house they professed to love. The house that bore God's name (which pagan nations saw as the symbol of Jewish faith) and the conduct of the people had become contrary to everything the house and the name of God should have represented.

The revival of faith begun by King Josiah simply had not gone deep enough. The people testified that they were "safe," but they did not show it in their lifestyle. They so admirably had restored the Temple, but they had stopped short of the religion of the heart. As every pastor knows, while it may be hard to raise money for a new building, it is far more difficult to raise hearts to a new level of dedication and spiritual sensitivity.

"Called by My Name"

Three times in this relatively short passage of Scripture we find the phrase "called by my name" describing the Temple, and verse 12 refers to the place where God made his name to dwell. In our society, where some people so easily take God's name in vain, we find it hard to understand this sense of reverence for God's name.

Not only did one of the commandments forbid the misuse of God's name, the people felt they should not speak the most sacred of the names for God at all, lest even in religious use they might say it too casually. Thus the unique significance of the Temple was not found in its magnificence or even in the fact that they built it according to a divinely revealed plan. The unique significance of the Temple was that it bore the name of God.

My soul responds to this reasoning. I once served as pastor of a United Methodist church that was called "The Church of the Saviour." From time to time I reminded my congregation that by belonging to a church with such a name, they had an awesome responsibility and must seek earnestly to live up to the name they bore. The members of every church could say the same. Being known as a Christian church means that the world around the building has the right to expect a great deal from that church.

Why do unchurched people expect church members to maintain a certain standard of community service and ethical conduct?

The Shiloh Warning

God had made his name "dwell at first" in Shiloh (Jeremiah 7:12). God now warned the people through Jeremiah that if they did not change their ways, he would do to this house that he gave to them and to their ancestors "just what I did to Shiloh" (7:14).

Shiloh was the place of worship for the Hebrews, beginning in the time of Joshua and continuing into that of the prophet Samuel. In fact, when he was a boy, Samuel lived at that temple, which housed the sacred ark of the covenant. When that earlier generation failed God and judgment fell, the Philistines destroyed Shiloh.

Jeremiah warned that just as God had allowed Shiloh to be destroyed, he could lift his hand and the same fate would befall Jerusalem. Such an idea was unthinkable for Jeremiah's contemporaries; yet only eighteen miles north of Jerusalem lay the ruins of Shiloh, mute evidence that it could, indeed, happen again.

Is such a warning applicable to your church? Why or why not?

Threat and Hope

The threat was fearful, and Jeremiah phrased it in unrelenting language. "I will cast you out of my sight, just as I cast out all your kinsfolk, all the offspring of Ephraim" (Jeremiah 7:15).

This language seems strong because we are so often inclined to make the love of God a weak, soft thing. The late Henry Sloane Coffin said that believers have discovered that "the grace of God . . . is not just a genial goodwill toward His creation. It is not God's good-naturedness. It is God giving Himself energetically to make out of those who let Him creators like Himself."[1] He went on to quote Martin Luther, that great advocate of the grace of God. "God's grace is something strong, mighty and busy; it is not something that lies inert in our souls."[2]

Yet if God's judgment contains a threat, still it implies mercy. Even the words of warning underline the pursuing love of God. "When I spoke to you persistently, you did not listen, and when I called you, you did not answer" (Jeremiah 7:13). I am awed by the way God so tirelessly follows after us human creatures. God speaks, and we do not listen; he calls, and we ignore his voice.

What evidence of God's love do you see in present-day instances of judgment?

What God Wanted

We can imagine the reaction of some earnest worshipers who were listening to Jeremiah as he stood at the gate of God's house. They probably were some of the best people in the land. They were good enough to "enter these gates to worship the Lord" (Jeremiah 7:2). Now they were hearing the prophet say, in God's stead, that they were violating God's house, making it a "den of robbers" (7:11). We could understand if one of them had said, "Just what does God expect of us! We've rebuilt the Temple, and we've torn down the places of idol worship. What more can God want?"

God's answer, through Jeremiah, was clear and strong. God wants righteous conduct, particularly as it relates to people other people often and easily oppress. Jeremiah listed especially the alien, the orphan, and the widow. These three groups constituted the persons society most often exploited and who were least able to defend themselves.

Jewish law was notable especially in defending the rights of the alien. The law always reminded the people that they were once strangers in the land of Egypt. As for the orphan and the widow, the most elementary human kindness should have compelled the people to care for them.

The Christian faith, to its credit, traditionally has made special provision for the orphan and the widow in our institutions of mercy, long before government agencies did so. We have not always been as sensitive to the needs of the alien. This insensitivity is ironic for most Americans, since most of us, through our ancestors, came to this land as aliens.

What God wanted, in other words, was for the people to live their faith rather than simply to mouth it. Pious phrases ("the temple of the LORD, the temple of the LORD") came so easily to their lips, as they do to ours. Upright conduct and daily compassion are not so easy to fulfill, however.

For Our Own Good

When you "go after other gods," Jeremiah warned, it is "to your own hurt" (Jeremiah 7:6). When we obey God's laws, we not only please him, we also assure ourselves a better life. Moral blindness makes us think we gain by mistreating others.

If we do what is right, the prophet said, God will "dwell with you in this place, in the land that I gave of old to your fathers forever and ever" (Jeremiah 7:7). Our personal life and our nation prosper when we live righteously.

Such righteousness, of course, is what God intends religion to produce. How tragic, then, that God's ancient people chose instead to use religion as a means of protecting themselves from God. Unfortunately, how little some of us seem to have learned from their example.

What opportunity do you have to practice practical religion in your personal setting?

CLOSING PRAYER
Save us, gracious God, from religion that uses ritual and dogma to hide us from reality and loving devotion. In Jesus' name we pray. Amen.

---

[1] From *Joy in Believing,* by Henry Sloane Coffin (Charles Scribner's Sons, 1956); page 125.
[2] From *Joy in Believing;* page 125.

Chapter Three

SUFFERING
FOR TRUTH

PURPOSE

To understand that believing in the truth and accepting it will sometimes bring suffering

BIBLE PASSAGE

Jeremiah 38:4-13

4 Then the officials said to the king, "This man ought to be put to death, because he is discouraging the soldiers who are left in this city, and all the people, by speaking such words to them. For this man is not seeking the welfare of this people, but their harm." 5 King Zedekiah said, "Here he is; he is in your hands; for the king is powerless against you." 6 So they took Jeremiah and threw him into the cistern of Malchiah, the king's son, which was in the court of the guard, letting Jeremiah down by ropes. Now there was no water in the cistern, but only mud, and Jeremiah sank in the mud.

7 Ebed-melech the Ethiopian, a eunuch in the king's house, heard that they had put Jeremiah into the cistern. The king happened to be sitting at the Benjamin Gate, 8 So Ebed-melech left the king's house and spoke to the king, 9 "My lord king, these men have acted wickedly in

all they did to the prophet Jeremiah by throwing him into the cistern to die there of hunger, for there is no bread left in the city." 10 Then the king commanded Ebed-melech the Ethiopian, "Take three men with you from here, and pull the prophet Jeremiah up from the cistern before he dies." 11 So Ebed-melech took the men with him and went to the house of the king, to a wardrobe of the storehouse, and took from there old rags and worn-out clothes, which he let down to Jeremiah in the cistern by ropes. 12 Then Ebed-melech the Ethiopian said to Jeremiah, "Just put the rags and clothes between your armpits and the ropes." Jeremiah did so. 13 Then they drew Jeremiah up by the ropes and pulled him out of the cistern. And Jeremiah remained in the court of the guard.

CORE VERSE
Blessed are those who are persecuted for righteousness' sake.
(Matthew 5:10)

OUR NEED

When a particular expression of truth becomes popular, people win favor and even political office by embracing it. Truth finds the best followers when it means persecution, however. Virtually every idea of any real merit passes through a period in which someone must pay the price of suffering.

We belong to a faith that has suffered persecution through most of the centuries of its history. "The more ye mow us down," Tertullian said, "the more we grow; the blood of the martyrs is the seed of the church." What Tertullian said early in the third century has continued to be true through the ages, even to the present time.

If we are to suffer for the truth, we must be committed to

it and convinced that we have found it. If suffering culminates in death, the worth of the truth has to be absolute.

Jeremiah paid such a price in order to deliver the message God had so deeply impressed on his heart. Clearly, Jeremiah felt the truth was worth the price.

FAITHFUL LIVING

Many prophets have had to deliver messages that offended their hearers. Few, however, have had as painful an assignment as the prophet Jeremiah.

It did not look that way at the outset. As we indicated earlier, Jeremiah began his ministry in the hopeful days of Josiah's reform. Yet after Josiah's death, twenty years passed under four kings who were in varying degrees both evil and inept. Meanwhile, the kingdom of Babylonia was solidifying its power.

The people of Judah saw the Babylonian menace, but they fooled themselves into believing that God would not allow a pagan foreign power to invade the land of his chosen people. Some false prophets were trying to subdue the fears of the people by promising peace (Jeremiah 6:14; 8:11). "There is no peace," Jeremiah declared. Instead, he warned, the Babylonians were going to invade their beloved land. Worse yet, the Babylonians were going to win. Worst of all, the people should cooperate with them. To oppose them would be to fight against God's purposes.

To understand Jeremiah's task in the simplest and clearest terms, we have to imagine a contemporary prophet announcing that a great power is soon to declare war on the United States, that this enemy will win, and that God wills it to be so. This kind of message does not gain favor for a preacher.

Jeremiah Stands Accused

We are not surprised to learn that the princes accused Jeremiah of being a traitor. A sentry arrested Jeremiah, saying, "You are deserting to the Chaldeans" (that is, the Babylonians) (Jeremiah 37:13). If you and I had lived in Judah at the time, we probably would have come to the same conclusion.

So the princes beat Jeremiah and threw him into prison. After he had been in a dungeon cell for "many days" (Jeremiah 37:16), he was called to an audience with King Zedekiah. The king asked him secretly, "Is there any word from the LORD?" (37:17).

This incident was a tribute to Jeremiah's integrity. The king and his court resented Jeremiah and his message of doom, yet Zedekiah somehow knew that Jeremiah spoke for God.

Perhaps Zedekiah also hoped that if he treated Jeremiah kindly, he would get a favorable message. Jeremiah's word was the same, however: "You shall be handed over to the king of Babylon" (Jeremiah 37:17). Then Jeremiah made a personal appeal: What wrong had he done to the king or to the nation that justified his punishment? Jeremiah was in the unhappy position of those who bring bad news; somehow the hearers hold the messengers partially responsible.

Zedekiah, whatever his other weaknesses, showed an element of kindness. Perhaps the measure of spiritual sensitivity that caused him to seek Jeremiah's opinion also was enough to make him protect Jeremiah from further harm. He arranged to send the prophet to the court of the guard, where the jailors provided him with a loaf of bread daily "until all the bread of the city was gone" (Jeremiah 37:21). A loaf of bread a day sounds like starvation fare to those of us who eat three meals a day, but one loaf of bread guaranteed continued existence in a city besieged.

Is it fair to blame the news media (our modern-day messengers) for the bad news they report? Why or why not?

Jeremiah's Bad News

Then God gave Jeremiah the most difficult message of all. He must tell the people that if they stayed in Jerusalem, they would die by sword, famine, and pestilence. If they wanted to live, they must go "out to the Chaldeans" (Jeremiah 38:2). Jeremiah announced, with unremitting certainty, "Thus says the LORD, This city shall surely be handed over to the army of the king of Babylon and be taken" (38:3).

Surely Jeremiah must have resisted giving this message. If I might put myself in his place, I imagine that he felt some tenderness toward King Zedekiah, who had befriended him. How could he now speak a word that would weaken Zedekiah still more? Jeremiah's role was something like that of a physician who is also a family friend and must give a fatal diagnosis. No wonder Jeremiah's ministry was bathed in tears!

We do not know if Zedekiah's patience was exhausted by this time, but it was too much for his princes. "This man ought to be put to death," they appealed to the king, "because he is discouraging the soldiers . . . and all the people" (Jeremiah 38:4). This conclusion was fair from their vantage point. Zedekiah answered, "Here he is; he is in your hands" (38:5).

So they took Jeremiah to the cistern of Malchiah and let him down by ropes. The cistern was without water, but Jeremiah "sank in the mud" (Jeremiah 38:6). I do not know if you and I really can imagine the pain and despair Jeremiah must have felt at this point.

When have you suffered for telling the truth?

Jeremiah's Deeper Pain

I am impressed that Jeremiah's deep cries of anguish did not come at his places of personal pain. We call him the "weeping" prophet, but his tears were not those of self-pity.

He cried, "Is there no balm in Gilead?" because he was dev-astated that "the health of my poor people" had not been restored (Jeremiah 8:22). When he prayed that his head might be "a spring of water" and his "eyes a fountain of tears," it was because he wanted to "weep day and night / for the slain of my poor people!" (9:1).

True, at one point Jeremiah almost was ready to give up his ministry. It seemed to him that God's word had made him a laughing stock. Yet when he resolved that he would not speak any more in God's name, he felt that "within me there is something like a burning fire / shut up in my bones" (Jeremiah 20:9). Perhaps the reason Jeremiah spent so little time pitying himself was because he was absorbed in hurting for God and for God's people. Self-pity is, after all, spiritually wrong. Pity should be directed outward, not inward.

When have you experienced pain because of someone else's pain?

Temporary Relief

As Jeremiah sank into the mud, help came from an unlikely source. That source was not one of his fellow Judahites but an Ethiopian eunuch, Ebed-melech, who worked in the king's house. When he heard that the princes had put Jere-miah into a cistern, he hurried to the king, who was at that moment sitting in the Benjamin Gate, perhaps trying to lift the morale of the people by his public appearance.

Ebed-melech warned the king that Jeremiah would die of hunger if he was left in the cistern and charged that the men had "acted wickedly" in putting him there (Jeremiah 38:9). Once again Zedekiah showed a humane streak. He ordered the Ethiopian to get three men and to lift Jeremiah out of the cistern without delay.

We realize the poverty that had come to Jerusalem in its

state of siege when we read the rescue method. Ebed-melech gathered "old rags and worn-out clothes" and let them down in the cistern by ropes, so Jeremiah could cushion his armpits for the rescue (Jeremiah 38:11). Jeremiah stayed in the court of the guard after the men delivered him from the cistern.

I marvel at the role of Ebed-melech. He is one of those hidden heroes of the Bible. Why was he sensitive to the prophet's need and courageous enough to plead his cause? Had he become convinced, somewhere along the way, of Jeremiah's integrity? He was not a Judahite, but he proved to be a better believer in God and his messenger than were many of God's chosen people. Ebed-melech was one of God's surprises. They appear at frequent and timely intervals throughout the Bible.

Whom do you view as one of God's surprises?

Conversation With Zedekiah

In a portion of Scripture beyond our Bible Passage, we learn that the king once again sought Jeremiah's counsel. "Do not hide anything from me," he pleaded (Jeremiah 38:14). Jeremiah, in turn, asked the king to guarantee his life; for he feared that if he spoke the truth to Zedekiah, he would pay with his blood.

With the king's assurance, the prophet told him that if he would surrender to the Babylonians, God would spare his life and not burn the city. Otherwise the Babylonians would capture him and destroy the city.

Zedekiah seemed to listen carefully; and to his credit he saw to it that Jeremiah's life was spared, as he had promised. He did not follow the prophet's counsel, however. When the Chaldeans marched in during the ninth year of his reign, he and his group resisted for a number of months; then they fled the city. The Chaldeans soon captured him, and the soldiers treated him brutally. They burned and ravished the city. The woes Jeremiah had predicted came true.

We are happy to read that Ebed-melech received his reward. Jeremiah sent a message from God to him. God promised that Ebed-melech would be saved "because you have trusted in me" (Jeremiah 39:18).

How do you explain people such as Zedekiah who hear the message of God but who do not respond positively?

Jeremiah's Continuing Work

The King of Babylonia saw to the preservation of Jeremiah's life. When Gedaliah became governor of the land, under King Nebuchadnezzar of Babylonia, it looked as if someone would take Jeremiah's counsel seriously. Soon, however, Gedaliah was assassinated; and again the people ignored Jeremiah's words. Nevertheless, Jeremiah continued to prophesy and to serve as spiritual counselor to the people of God.

We are perplexed somewhat at Jeremiah's ministry. The times he lived in were trying, and his own life was marked by public rejection and private pain. By the usual measure of things, his ministry was a failure.

The Challenge to Be Faithful

Jeremiah was not the first person or the last to live under such circumstances. Some generations, as President Franklin Roosevelt said, seem to have a rendezvous with destiny. Others dwell in quiet times.

We all wish that we might live in days of sunshine and peace. Nevertheless, we must acknowledge that some of the happiest and most productive people have fulfilled their calling in days when the tide of personal or public history went outward.

Whatever the times or circumstances, however, the Christian knows that his or her calling is to be faithful. We are not captive to our times. We live in the midst of history, but we are not subject to it. Our allegiance is to God, not to the passing events of history.

I believe that God will judge us according to our faithfulness in the times in which we live. It is more difficult to live in an age of persecution; but the spiritual perils of times of prosperity may be more hazardous still.

Jesus said that the requirements of stewards are that they be faithful. That requirement is the same whether the steward has one talent or ten, whether he or she struggles for bare subsistence in a relocation center or lives in a comfortable suburb. I take both comfort and discomfort in the knowledge that God is a righteous judge who knows the right measure of faithfulness in the settings in which you and I live.

Jeremiah was faithful to the truth, and he suffered for it. Perhaps the one advantage he had over many of us is that for him the lines were drawn sharply. Our decisions usually are not so incisive or our choices marked so clearly. A king does not call us to account for our words. We might wish, at times, that our decisions had more heroic proportions so that we would know the significance of the will of God.

Whatever the circumstance, God calls us to be faithful even at the cost of suffering.

What challenges do you encounter in your daily walk of faith?

CLOSING PRAYER

God of all mercy, grant us the strength to be true to you in good days and in bad, in grand decisions and in petty moments, and always to your glory. In Jesus' name we pray. Amen.

Chapter Four

A NEW COVENANT

PURPOSE

To rejoice in God's new covenant, which is written on the human heart, bringing forgiveness of sins and new and eternal life

BIBLE PASSAGE

Jeremiah 31:27-34

27 The days are surely coming, says the LORD, when I will sow the house of Israel and the house of Judah with the seed of humans and the seed of animals. 28 And just as I have watched over them to pluck up and break down, to overthrow, destroy, and bring evil, so I will watch over them to build and to plant, says the LORD. 29 In those days they shall no longer say:

"The parents have eaten sour grapes,
and the children's teeth are set on edge."

30 But all shall die for their own sins; the teeth of everyone who eats sour grapes shall be set on edge.

31 The days are surely coming, says the LORD, when I will make a new covenant with the house of Israel and the house of Judah. 32 It will not be like the covenant that I made

with their ancestors when I took them by the hand to bring them out of the land of Egypt—a covenant that they broke, though I was their husband, says the LORD. 33 But this is the covenant that I will make with the house of Israel after those days, says the LORD: I will put my law within them, and I will write it on their hearts; and I will be their God, and they shall be my people. 34 No longer shall they teach one another, or say to each other, "Know the LORD," for they shall all know me, from the least of them to the greatest, says the LORD; for I will forgive their iniquity, and remember their sin no more.

CORE VERSE
I will put my law within them, and I will write it on their hearts; and I will be their God, and they shall be my people.
(Jeremiah 31:33)

OUR NEED

Again and again, in symbols, predictions, and promises, the Hebrew Scriptures tell us that a new and better day is coming. No one spoke of a better day more emphatically than did the prophet Jeremiah. Isaiah probably is the Old Testament prophet we quote most frequently and whose words come alive to us especially at Christmas and during Holy Week. Jeremiah, however, announced the most distinctly that a new time was coming.

As a result, we sometimes refer to Jeremiah's book as "the gospel before the gospel." With a burst of hope, Jeremiah predicted the coming of a new covenant. We recognize it as the covenant that has come to us in Jesus Christ.

FAITHFUL LIVING

When God called Jeremiah to be a prophet, God told him that his ministry would be

> to pluck up and to pull down,
> to destroy and to overthrow,
> to build and to plant.
> (Jeremiah 1:10)

Jeremiah could have complained that he gave most of his time and message to the breaking and destroying portion of his assignment. The time came, however, when he was privileged to build and to plant; and he did so in a way that made him distinctive among the Old Testament prophets. Others seemed to anticipate a new era, but no one was able to declare it in such direct and unmistakable language as Jeremiah.

Time for the New?

It was not an auspicious time for the birth of the new. Jeremiah was prophesying in a time of national decline, just as the Babylonians were about to overwhelm his beloved people and a pagan army was about to destroy the Holy City.

Yet, who can say when the time is right for the new to come or to be announced? We may even hear the challenge of the new most clearly when the old is beginning to crumble around us. In the midst of such a dark time, Jeremiah received a vision of a better day that was beyond anything his people had ever known.

In what way is our time ready for a new word from God?

An Old Law Turned Around

The Hebrew people had a profound sense of collective responsibility. They had more of this sense, in fact, than we can understand easily, geared as we are to a philosophy of individualism. They saw themselves more as a people than as individuals, and they had an almost mystical belief in the effect of one generation on another.

The people had a popular proverb: "The parents have eaten sour grapes, / and the children's teeth are set on edge" (Jeremiah 31:29). Their belief was more than that of one generation paying for the mistakes of the previous one; it was an affirmation of the principle of solidarity in the human race.

Jeremiah declared that this age-old rule would be true no longer. "But all," he said, "shall die for their own sins; the teeth of everyone who eats sour grapes shall be set on edge" (Jeremiah 31:30). Each individual must bear responsibility for himself or herself.

A New Covenant

The Old Testament is an account of a series of covenants between God and the patriarchs, culminating in the covenant with the Hebrew nation. In many ways, the recurring theme of the prophets was a call to the nation to live up to the covenant God had made with them. The focal point of that covenant was the law, the honored possession of the Hebrew people.

Proud as the people were of the law, however, they did not necessarily fulfill its demands. To use an old saying, they observed it more in the breach than in the doing.

So God announced through Jeremiah that he was going to give Israel and Judah a new covenant. We might consider this announcement an admission that the old covenant had failed. I think the apostle Paul would say that it had done all it was intended to do. Paul said that the law was to prepare the world for Christ (Galatians 3:24).

The relationship of God with the people authenticated the law. Exodus 20 begins, "I am the LORD your God, who brought you out of the land of Egypt, out of the house of slavery; you shall have no other gods before me" (verses 2-3).

God had a right to call for a covenant because he had delivered this people.

G. Campbell Morgan, a Bible expositor early in the previous century, said that the law was never given to the people until they had found God. This order of things has a reason. "All written laws fail," Morgan writes, "because within human personality there is something infinitely greater than ever can be conditioned within any law uttered at a single moment."[1] So God needed a new covenant, one that went beyond words, structures, and organizations and that dealt with the deepest core of the person.

Why is it true in all our human relationships, as in our relationship with God, that the better we know the person, the better we fulfill the demands of the relationship?

An Expression of Hope

Jeremiah so easily and so justifiably could have lost all confidence in his people. The religious revival that began so hopefully in his youth had faded. The kings were inept, and the people responded foolishly to lying prophets. The situation seemed to have been this way for generations.

Yet Jeremiah somehow believed that the people were capable of responding to God and that they could change. He makes me think of the teacher who taught our class of boys when I was thirteen or fourteen. We boys often were thoughtless of her and inexcusably impolite. Yet she somehow always seemed to believe that we would turn out all right and that we were worth the effort she put into teaching. Daily she came to class with her earnestly prepared lesson—and usually also with a box of fudge to pass among us as the class hour ended, a special treat in the days of the Great Depression! She believed we could be the people of God.

Apparently Jeremiah felt that way, too. As a result, he

dared to promise a new covenant to his people. If he had not possessed such a vigorous faith, I think he would have said, "Why bother?" He believed in the grace of God, however; and he believed that the people were capable of responding to such grace.

The Man and the Message

Jeremiah's faith was consistent with his whole character. Professor Lindsay Longacre said that Jeremiah embodied the Beatitudes of the Sermon on the Mount better than any other Old Testament character. Professor Longacre compared Jeremiah with Jesus, noting that both men came under popular condemnation for predicting the destruction of the Temple, both stirred up the hatred of the official priesthood, and both were put to death by the people they were trying to help. Jeremiah referred to himself as a lamb led to the slaughter (Jeremiah 11:19), a phrase we find in Isaiah 53:7 and that the New Testament applies to Jesus.

A message has its greatest impact when it is consistent with the personality of the speaker. Jeremiah had the inner integrity to give power to the words that he spoke. No wonder God entrusted him with the proclamation of the coming of the new era!

In what way can your words have power?

The Heart of the Matter

What would work with this wayward people, if even so grand a document as the law was not enough? The secret, Jeremiah knew, was in the human heart. "I will put my law within them, and I will write it on their hearts" (Jeremiah 31:33).

If the covenant was to succeed, it had to be ever-present. When God gave the law to Moses, the people were told to bind the law for a sign upon the hand and as "an emblem on your forehead" and to write it on the doorposts of their homes and on their gates as a constant reminder of their commitment (Deuteronomy 6:8-9).

Yet even these physical reminders were not enough, because they were external. If we do not control our thoughts and our affections, we can read the right words at every turn and still go the wrong way. We must have a deeper quickening of memory.

Physical symbols are not enough unless we have a commitment within. We may wear or carry a pretty cross, and we may dot the walls of our rooms with Scripture verses; yet we may be indifferent to God. The law, Jeremiah said, must be written within us if it is to fulfill its purposes.

What role do religious symbols play in your life?

The Hardest Substance

Jeremiah was no easy sentimentalist. The Mosaic law had been engraved on tables of stone, but Jeremiah recognized that the heart is an even tougher substance. "The heart is deceitful above all things," he said, "and desperately wicked: who can know it?" (Jeremiah 17:9, KJV).

We have made the heart such a warm and sentimental symbol that the words of the prophet are likely to shock us. Our bumper stickers use a heart as a substitute for the word *love,* with the object of the verb being anything from a favorite pet to a city or a vacation spot. Jeremiah would argue with that heart symbol. He would tell us that a heart can stand as easily for hate as it does for love. In fact, he might assert that the product of the heart was more likely to be hate than love. Jeremiah knew that if God were to engrave his new covenant on the heart, he would have to have a piercing stylus and a strong hand.

Once an impression is made on the heart, it is part of the

most vital place. We think of the heart as the seat of the emotions, but it was significantly more than that to the Hebrews. When they wanted to refer to the emotions, they would speak of the bowels, as we sometimes say that we feel something in the pit of our stomach. The heart represented thought as well as emotion. The heart was emotion with the quality of intelligence.

"Their God . . . My People"

The aim of the Mosaic covenant was that the Hebrews would be God's people. Now Jeremiah declared that the glorious goal of the new covenant was that "I will be their God, and they shall be my people" (Jeremiah 31:33). The union had a different quality because now it was a personal commitment (Jeremiah 31:34) rather than a national, corporate bond. The covenant had become a law of the heart rather than a law of stone.

We must note another strategic point also. God promised the people, "I will forgive their iniquity, and remember their sin no more" (Jeremiah 31:34). This covenant was based on a restored relationship for a forgiven people. God gave the law to a nation that God delivered from the bondage of Egypt. God offered the new covenant to those people who accepted deliverance from the bondage of sin.

The Covenant Today

What about you and me? God still calls us to give our heart to God. The love God demonstrated at Calvary demands our heart in return. To respond to God's supreme love with less than our heart is blasphemy.

I expect that on the basis of that kind of thinking, John Wesley, the founder of Methodism, wrote a covenant service that pledged,

Lord, make me what you will.
I put myself fully into your hands:

put me to doing, put me to suffering,
let me be employed for you, or laid aside for you,
let me be full, let me be empty,
let me have all things, let me have nothing.
I freely and with a willing heart
give it all to your pleasure and disposal.[2]

How do you give your heart to God?

CLOSING PRAYER
Take your place in our hearts, dear Savior, that we may
be wholly, lovingly yours this day. In Jesus' name we pray.
Amen.

---

[1] From *Studies in the Prophecy of Jeremiah,* by G. Campbell Morgan (Fleming
H. Revell Co., 1931); page 181.
[2] From *The United Methodist Book of Worship* [Copyright © 1992 The United
Methodist Publishing House]; page 291. Used by permission.